Elementary Language Arts
Semester B

2nd GRADE

ACCELERATE EDUCATION

Contents

Write the Passage with Pronouns

Rewrite the passage with pronouns.

Brian and Loreen saw the green ball in the corner, but Sonia saw it too. "The turn belongs to us to play ball," said Brian. "No," said Randy. "The turn belongs to Sonia. " It is a ball that belongs to her. "Brian and I saw the ball first," said Loreen. "It is a ball that belongs to us."

"Loreen, Sonia, and I can share the ball," said Brian.

Rewrite:

_____

- -

_____

_____

- -

_____

_____

- -

_____

_____

- -

_____

_____

- -

_____

_____

- -

_____

My name is: _____

Foods That You Don't Like

Name of Food:	Why You Don't Like It:

Personal and Possessive Pronouns

Circle the possessive pronouns and underline the personal pronouns.

Carla likes to make a prickly pear smoothie. It is cold and refreshing. She makes them with her mother. It is their favorite snack on a hot day. Carla said to her brother, "I will make a smoothie for you. It will become your favorite thing to drink." She put vanilla flavor in his smoothie. It is his favorite flavor.

Write your own passage with personal and possessive pronouns below.

Name _____.

Spelling Test

Directions: As your teacher reads your words, write each spelling word on the blanks below.

1) _____

2) _____

3) _____

4) _____

5) _____

6) _____

7) _____

8) _____

9) _____

10) _____

11) _____

12) _____

13) _____

14) _____

15) _____

My name is: _____

Favorite Foods Story Map

WHO: _____

_____

WHERE: _____

_____

WHAT:

EVENT #1: _____

_____

_____

EVENT #2: _____

_____

_____

EVENT #3: _____

_____

_____

PROBLEM:

_____

_____

_____

_____

_____

SOLUTION:

_____

_____

_____

_____

_____

PROBLEM:

_____

_____

_____

_____

_____

SOLUTION:

_____

_____

_____

_____

_____

Reflexive Pronouns

Directions:
Use the reflexive pronouns in the word bank to complete each sentence. A reflexive pronoun is when a noun or pronoun is doing something to itself.

myself	themselves
herself	yourself
ourselves	himself
	itself

1. Be careful you do not hurt _____ riding the bike.

2. Greg asked to build the block tower by _____.

3. I wrote a note to remind _____ about my appointment.

4. The girls on the team are practicing to better _____ before the competition.

5. We heard _____ singing on the radio last week.

6. The rabbit fed _____ carrots from our garden.

7. Cheryl was proud of _____ for earning a good grade on the test.

Name: _____

Animal Jobs

What is a job that people do with animals? _____

Directions:
Complete the boxes below by listing details about the job.

Animals:	Responsibilities:

Tools:	Location:

Other (Education/Pay/Etc.):

Name _____.

Spelling Test

Directions: As your teacher reads your words, write each spelling word on the blanks below.

1) _____

2) _____

3) _____

4) _____

5) _____

6) _____

7) _____

8) _____

9) _____

10) _____

11) _____

12) _____

13) _____

14) _____

15) _____

Finding Text Evidence

Directions:
Fill in the empty boxes with evidence from the story to support each sentence.

Statement: Example: Bobby and Pixie were dirty in the beginning of the story.	**Evidence:** Example: Bobby's hair was full of sand and dust. Pixie left bits of sand and grass behind.
Statement: 1.) Bobby and Pixie were excited when they first saw Susan get two leashes.	**Evidence:**
Statement: 2.) Pixie liked having a bath.	**Evidence:**
Statement: 3.) Bobby and Pixie were dirty at the end of the story.	**Evidence :**

Name: _____

Lost and Found

Brainstorm a problem: _____.

Directions: Complete the boxes below. Draw a picture of the problem and solution/solutions. Then, write about the problem and solution/solutions.

Problem- Illustration	Solution- Illustration
Problem- What is it? List details.	**Solution-** How can you solve the problem? List details.

Phonics

Directions:
Use the words in the word bank to complete the sentences.

WORD BANK:
yard   hard   far
darkness barked
park   farm   carpet
party   sharp

1. We went to the _____ to look at the goats.

2. Do you want to have a picnic in the _____?

3. Please do not wear your shoes on the _____.

4. We are going outside to play in the _____.

5. You can send emails if you live _____ away.

6. The _____ of the night added to the scary movie.

7. The dog _____ when it was hungry.

8. It is _____ to learn to tie your shoes.

9. I will have a birthday _____ next month.

10. Please be careful with the _____ knife.

Name _____.

Spelling Test

Directions: As your teacher reads your words, write each spelling word on the blanks below.

1) _____

2) _____

3) _____

4) _____

5) _____

6) _____

7) _____

8) _____

9) _____

10) _____

11) _____

12) _____

13) _____

14) _____

15) _____

Name: _____

Finding Text Evidence

Directions:
Fill in the empty boxes with evidence from the story to support each sentence.

Statement: Example: It was raining at the beginning of the story.	**Evidence:** Example: The front yard was full of water. The back yard was full of water. It was still raining in the beginning of the story.
Statement: 1.) Pippi looked for Franky.	**Evidence:**
Statement: 2.) The crawl space was dark and wet.	**Evidence:**
Statement: 3.) Pippi, Pixie, and Bobby helped rescue Franky.	**Evidence :**

Name:_____

Good and Bad Habits

Name of Person	Describe Good Habits	Describe Bad Habits

COMPREHENSION

Read and take notes.
1. Circle words that you do not know.
2. Underline phrases that help and phrases that you don't understand.
3. Write thoughts or questions in the margins.

WHERE OLD MR. GOBBLER GOT THE STRUTTING HABIT

The Gobblers never have gotten over strutting since Old Mr. Gobbler, the first of the family, got the habit.

"Tell me about it. Please, Grandfather Frog, tell me about it," begged Peter. "How did Old Mr. Gobbler get the habit?"

Grandfather Frog chuckled. "He got it from admiring his own reflection in a pool of water," said he. "You see, in those days way back when the world was young, people had more time to form habits than they do now. With plenty to eat and little to do, they had more time to think about themselves than they do now. Old Mr. Gobbler soon discovered that he was the biggest of all of the birds in that part of the Great World where he lived, and this discovery was, I suspect, the beginning of his vanity. then one day as he was walking along, he came to a little pool of water. It was very clear, and there wasn't a ripple on the surface. There for the first time Mr. Gobbler saw his reflection. The more he looked, the better he liked his own appearance. He spread his tail just to see how it would look in the water. Then he puffed himself out and strutted.

"'There is nobody to compare with me,' thought he, and strutted more than ever."

Name _____.

Spelling Test

Directions: As your teacher reads your words, write each spelling word on the blanks below.

1) _____

2) _____

3) _____

4) _____

5) _____

6) _____

7) _____

8) _____

9) _____

10) _____

11) _____

12) _____

13) _____

14) _____

15) _____

Name: _____

Writing Graphic Organizer

Directions:
Use the lines to brainstorm topics for each paragraph. Complete the boxes with details for each paragraph.

Paragraph Ideas:
Clothes, education, setting of work, clients/customers, responsibilities.

The community job I will write about is: _____.

Topic of First Paragraph: _____.

First Paragraph- Details:

continued on next page...

Topic of Second Paragraph: _____.

Second Paragraph- Details:

Topic of Third Paragraph: _____.

Third Paragraph- Details:

Name: _____

Spelling Worksheet

Directions: Complete the table using your spelling words.

Adjectives (Positive)	Comparative Adjectives	Superlative Adjectives
Short		

Directions: Create a sentence for the following spelling words.

1. easy

2. worse

3. exam

4. waiting

Name _____.

Spelling Test

Directions: As your teacher reads your words, write each spelling word on the blanks below.

1) _____

2) _____

3) _____

4) _____

5) _____

6) _____

7) _____

8) _____

9) _____

10) _____

11) _____

12) _____

13) _____

14) _____

15) _____

Finding Text Evidence

Directions:
Fill in the empty boxes with evidence from the story to support each sentence.

Statement:
Example: Pixie was happy when her ear was all better.

Evidence:
Example: Pixie wagged her tail. She ran in circles chasing her tail because she was happy.

Statement:
1.) Pixie's ear was bothering her at the beginning of the story.

Evidence:

Statement:
2.) Dr. Kirk gave directions and care for Pixie's ear.

Evidence:

Statement:
3.) Pixie did not want her ear to be cleaned.

Evidence:

Name: _____

Brainstorm Organizer

Directions: Write your problem and solution for our descriptive paragraphs. Draw pictures and list adjectives and adverbs that tell about your problem and solution.

The problem will be _____.

Draw a picture of the problem. Use colors and add small details in your drawing.

What are some adjectives to describe your problem?

_____

What are some adverbs to describe your problem?

_____

continued on the next page:

The solution will be _____.

Draw a picture of the solution. Use colors and add small details in your drawing.

What are some adjectives to describe your solution?
_____

What are some adverbs to describe your solution?
_____

Adverbs

Directions:
Adverbs describe verbs. They tell us when, where, why, how often, and to what extent something happened. Find the adverb and verb in each sentence.

Circle the adverb. Underline the verb it modifies or describes.

1.) My dad left early.

2.) I completely understand my math homework.

3.) The little girl walked slowly.

4.) Ted ran quickly.

5.) Sophia dances gracefully.

6.) Mom carefully placed the vase of flowers on the bookcase.

7.) The boy waited calmly.

8.) She eagerly raised her hand to participate.

9.) The student politely asked a question.

10.) Dad carefully carried the glasses.

Name: _____

Spelling

Directions: Write the spelling word. Then create a sentence using the spelling word.

Spelling Word: beautifully	Write Word:

Sentence: _____

_____

Spelling Word: suddenly	Write Word:

Sentence: _____

_____

Spelling Word: slowly	Write Word:

Sentence: _____

_____

Spelling Word: swiftly	Write Word:

Sentence: _____

_____

Spelling Word: angrily	Write Word:

Sentence: _____

_____

Spelling Word: quickly	Write Word:

Sentence: _____

_____

continued on the next page:

Spelling Word: greedily	Write Word:

Sentence: _____

_____

Spelling Word: fast	Write Word:

Sentence: _____

_____

Spelling Word: less	Write Word:

Sentence: _____

_____

Spelling Word: more	Write Word:

Sentence: _____

_____

Spelling Word: merrily	Write Word:

Sentence: _____

_____

Spelling Word: bouquet	Write Word:

Sentence: _____

_____

Spelling Word: flowers	Write Word:

Sentence: _____

_____

continued on the next page:

Spelling Word: stalks	Write Word:

Sentence: _____

_____

Spelling Word: feathers	Write Word:

Sentence: _____

_____

Name _____.

Spelling Test

Directions: As your teacher reads your words, write each spelling word on the blanks below.

1) _____

2) _____

3) _____

4) _____

5) _____

6) _____

7) _____

8) _____

9) _____

10) _____

11) _____

12) _____

13) _____

14) _____

15) _____

Name: _____

Making Mischief

I learned to be responsible from a mistake when:

Directions: Draw a picture in each box:

Beginning: What I already knew...	Middle: How I did not follow the rule...	End: How I learned from my mistake...

Directions: Write down information describing the picture in each box. Remember to use adjectives and adverbs

Beginning	Middle	End

Making Mischief Spelling

Directions: Use the words in the word bank to complete each sentence.

WORD BANK:

tooth	caught	draw
person	knife	cage
people	knives	touch
catch	drew	teeth

1. The sign for the dentist has a large _____ on it.

2. My _____ are shiny and white.

3. Can you _____ a cat?

4. Last week, he _____ a rainbow with chalk.

5. I need a _____ to cut my sandwich.

6. My mom bought my dad a new set of _____.

7. Sammy went to the batting _____ to practice hitting the ball.

8. Did you _____ a cold?

9. Last year, I _____ the flu.

10. My little sister is not allowed to _____ anything in the cabinets.

11. There was one _____ waiting in the room.

12. Most _____ schedule their dentist appointment for earlier in the day.

continued on next page...

Directions: Create a sentence for the following words:

13. child

_____

~~~~~~

_____

~~~~~~

14. children

_____

~~~~~~

_____

~~~~~~

15. badge

_____

~~~~~~

_____

~~~~~~

Spelling Test

Spelling

Directions: As your teacher reads your words, write each spelling word on the blanks below.

1) _____

2) _____

3) _____

4) _____

5) _____

6) _____

7) _____

8) _____

9) _____

10) _____

11) _____

12) _____

13) _____

14) _____

15) _____

Name: _____

Writing Brainstorm:
Complete the boxes below. Use a separate sheet of paper to continue the content sections as needed.

FORMAL EMAIL:

Body: Use large words. No abbreviations, slang or contractions.

🗐 New Message	_ ☐ ✕

File Edit View Insert Format Tools Message Help

Send Cut Copy Paste Undo Check Spelling Attach Priority Sign

To: _____@mail.com

Cc: _____

Subject: What happened at the zoo?

Arial   10   B I U A

Greeting: _____

Content:

_____
_____
_____
_____
_____

Closing:_____

_____

INFORMAL EMAIL:

Body: Use small words, abbreviations, slang or contractions.

```
New Message                                                    _ □ ✕

 File   Edit   View   Insert   Format   Tools   Message   Help        ⊞

  ⇥        ✂        ⬚        ⬚        ↶       👤      ABC✓     📎      ↓!  ▾    ⬚
 Send      Cut     Copy    Paste    Undo    Check   Spelling  Attach  Priority   Sign

 📖 To:   _____@mail.com

 📖 Cc:   _____

 Subject: What happened at the zoo?

 Arial             ▾  10 ▾   ⬚▾  B  I  U  A▾  ⬚ ⬚ ⬚ ⬚  ⬚ ⬚ ⬚ ⬚  — 🎨
```

Greeting: _____

Content:

_____

_____

_____

_____

_____

Closing:_____

_____

Name _____.

Spelling Test

Directions: As your teacher reads your words, write each spelling word on the blanks below.

1) _____

2) _____

3) _____

4) _____

5) _____

6) _____

7) _____

8) _____

9) _____

10) _____

11) _____

12) _____

13) _____

14) _____

15) _____

Name: _____

Franky Goes Fishing

Directions:
Compare and contrast Franky and the fish from our story by completing the Venn diagram.

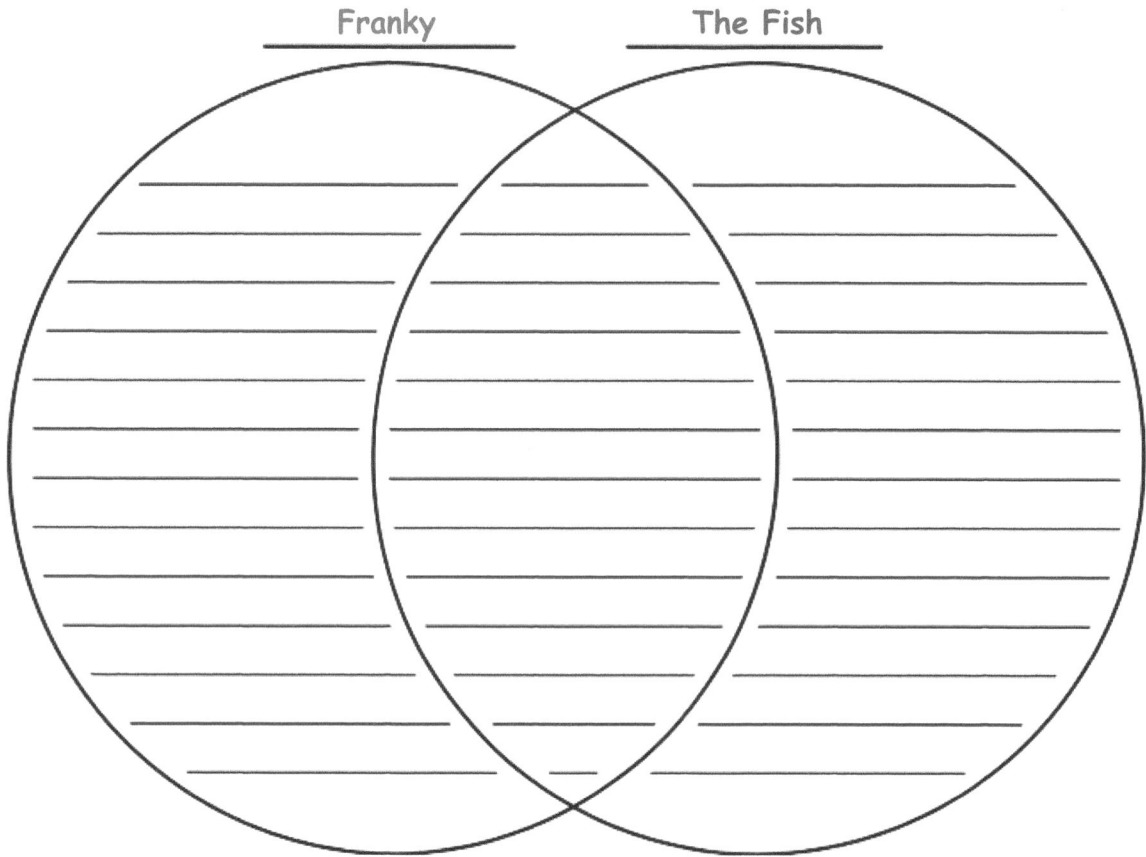

Franky   The Fish

Name: _____

Animal Adventures

Directions: Write the rule for a comma in the first column. List examples to prove the rule in the second column.

Rules	Examples of Proof
1.	
2.	
3.	
4.	
5.	
6.	
7.	
8.	

Name: _____

Animal Adventures

Directions: Complete the boxes by following the directions next to each.

Heading: Write the address of the person you are writing the letter to. This can be made up. Write the date underneath the address.

Greeting: Write a greeting or introduction and the name of the person. Example: Dear Mrs. Smith,

Body: Write the paragraphs about your move below.

Closing and Signature: Write a word or two to say goodbye. Sign your name underneath.
Example: Sincerely, Tom Smith

Name _____.

Letter Organization

Identify the parts of a letter using the word bank to the right. Write your answers beneath the word bank.

①
110 Street Road
Princeton, New Jersey 08540
July 21, 2014

Dear Kevin, ②

    This has been a great trip! This month we have traveled to California, Arizona, and Hawaii. While tiring, it has been lots of fun.

    My favorite state was Hawaii. Sharon says, "The volcanoes were spectacular!" We were able to stand far away and watch as a small volcano had lava flowing into the ocean. It was scary but exciting at the same time.

    Arizona was unbearably hot during the day. However, the nights ③ were chilly. We even used sweatshirts to keep warm at night.

    In California we met a bear, Fred, at the San Diego Zoo. He was a large grizzly bear. We watched him eat lunch and walk around for a few minutes. I was nervous, but there was strong glass to protect us.

    It is hard to believe this trip is coming to an end. We will be back in New Jersey on Friday. I will call you when we land. I plan to show you lots of pictures!

Love, ④

Katie Smith ⑤

Body
Signature
Heading
Greeting
Closing

1. _____

2. _____

3. _____

4. _____

5. _____

Animal Adventures
Crossword Puzzle

Directions: Complete the crossword puzzle using our vocabulary words.

ACROSS:
2   Goodbye
4   Used to say something is accurate, complete or correct
5   Almost but not quite
6   In different ways

DOWN:
1   To make believe
3   A light, strong substance that can be made into shapes

Name: _____

Animal Adventures

Directions: Create a sentence to show the slight difference in meaning in many of our spelling words.

Spelling Word:	Sentence:
toss	
throw	
hurl	
thin	
slender	
skinny	
terrible	
awful	
horrible	
stroll	
tiptoe	
stride	
lady	
pilot	
music	

Name _____.

Spelling Test

Directions: As your teacher reads your words, write each spelling word on the blanks below.

1) _____

2) _____

3) _____

4) _____

5) _____

6) _____

7) _____

8) _____

9) _____

10) _____

11) _____

12) _____

13) _____

14) _____

15) _____

Name: _____

Animal Adventure

Directions:
Pick a character from our characterization worksheet. Choose another animal character that you know well. This can be a fairy tale animal or an animal character or from a different story you have read. Compare and contrast the two characters. Write the name of each character on the lines above each circle. Remember, the section where the circles overlap are is where to list what both characters have in common.

Patterns

Directions:
Complete the boxes below on your favorite subject.

My Opinion/ Main Idea:

Detail 1:

Detail 2:

Detail 3:

Closing Sentence / Restate Main Idea:

Patterns
Spelling

Directions:
Complete the boxes below on your favorite subject.

Word Bank

question	adventure
furniture	vacation
direction	location
figure	action
nature	picture
reflection	addition
subtraction	moisture
feature	

E=MC²

Suffix -tion

Suffix -ture or -ure

Name _____.

Spelling Test

Directions: As your teacher reads your words, write each spelling word on the blanks below.

1) _____

2) _____

3) _____

4) _____

5) _____

6) _____

7) _____

8) _____

9) _____

10) _____

11) _____

12) _____

13) _____

14) _____

15) _____

Name: _____

Patterns
Reading

Directions:
Using the paragraphs in our lesson, write the
main idea and details from each paragraph below.

Paragraph 1

Main Idea:	
Detail 1:	
Detail 2:	
Detail 3:	

Paragraph 2

Main Idea:	
Detail 1:	
Detail 2:	
Detail 3:	

Name: _____

Planet Earth

Brainstorm: Write your main idea in the middle circle.
Research and write details in the circles around
the main idea.

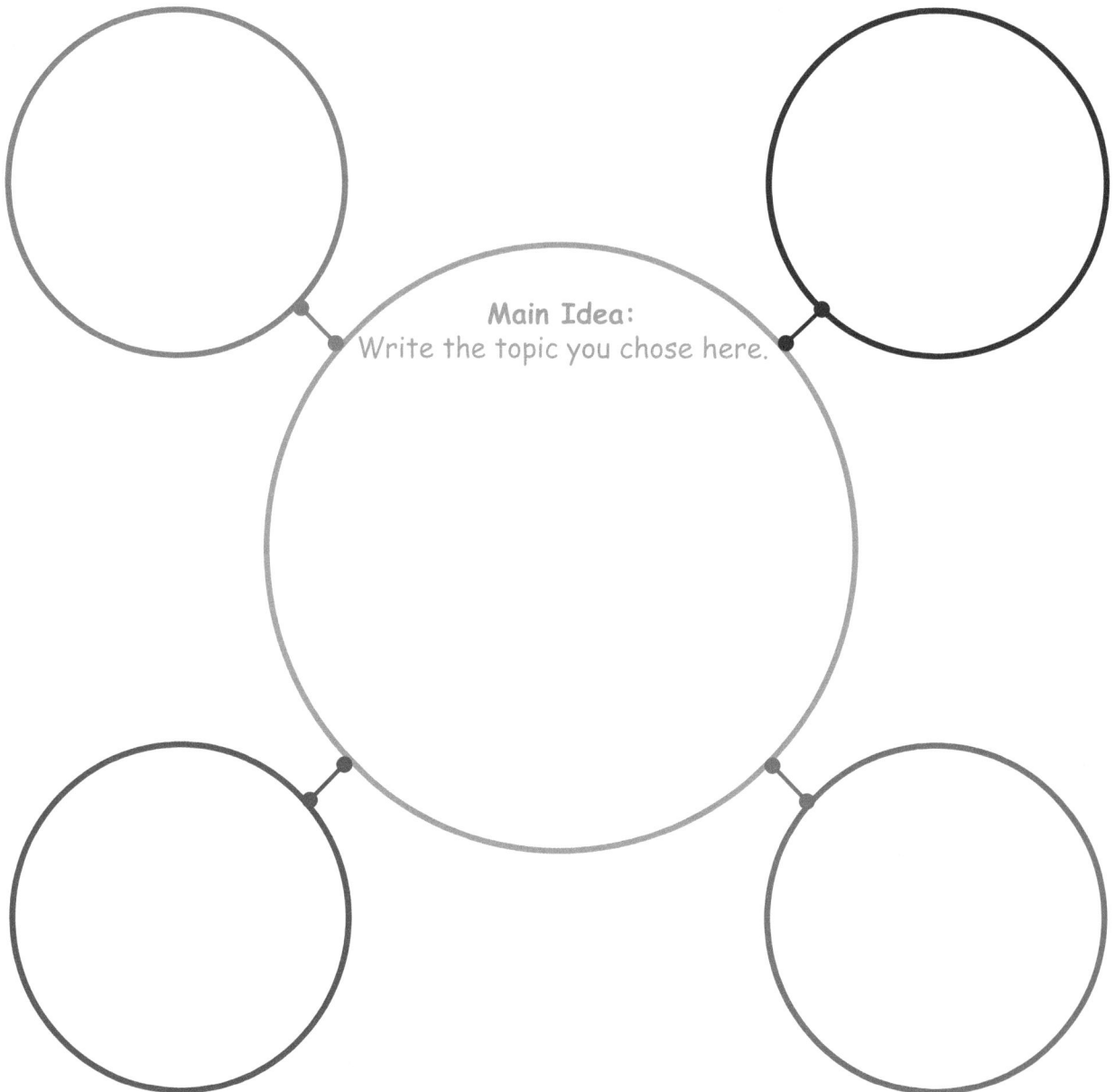

Main Idea:
Write the topic you chose here.

Name: _____

Planet Earth
Reading Worksheet

Directions:
Write what you think you know about our reading story this week. Then, write what you want to learn about our topic. After reading the story, come back and write what you have learned.

Know: What do you know about Earth?	Want: What do you want to learn about our planet?	Learn: What did you learn after reading our story?

Planet Earth
Spelling Worksheet

Directions:
Complete the table using your spelling words with prefixes.
Then, write sentences using your vocabulary spelling words.

Prefix	Base Word	Spelling Word
Example: re	use	reuse
1.		
2.		
3.		
4.		
5.		
6.		
7.		
8.		
9.		
10.		

Name _____.

Spelling Test

Directions: As your teacher reads your words, write each spelling word on the blanks below.

1) _____

2) _____

3) _____

4) _____

5) _____

6) _____

7) _____

8) _____

9) _____

10) _____

11) _____

12) _____

13) _____

14) _____

15) _____

Name:_____

Water

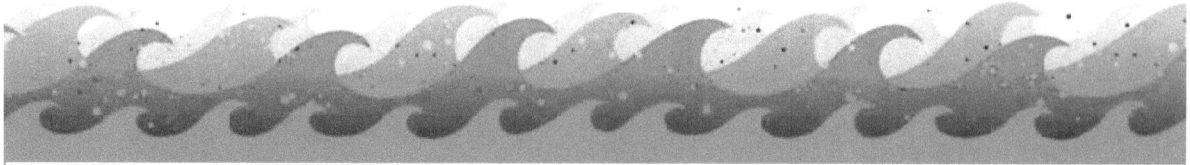

Topic: Conserve Water _____

_____

_____

Main Idea: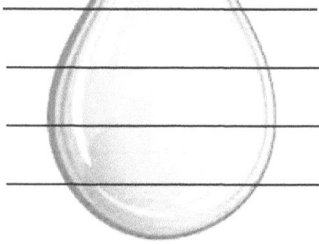

Main Idea: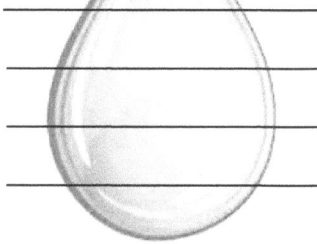

Main Idea: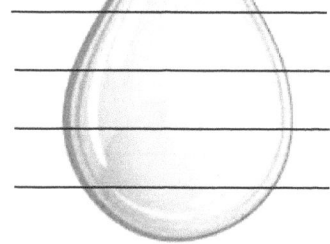

Details:	Details:	Details:

Name:_____

Water

Directions:
Write your spelling words in the correct category based on the spelling pattern. Underline the spelling pattern in each word.

-al	-au	-aw

Water
Grammar

Directions:
Rewrite each example of informal language as formal language.

1. Hey, what's up?

   _____
   -
   _____
   _____
   -
   _____

2. Turn that horrible racket off!

   _____
   -
   _____
   _____
   -
   _____

3. Want to catch a movie?

   _____
   -
   _____
   _____
   -
   _____

continue to next page...

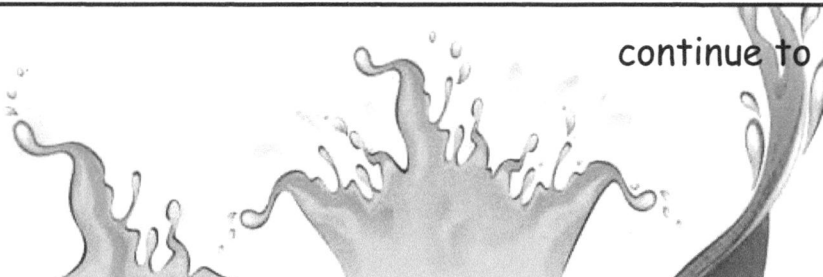

Directions:
Rewrite each example of formal language as informal language.

4. Could you please pass the mashed potatoes?

_____
- -
_____
_____
- -
_____

5. Goodbye. I look forward to our next meeting.

_____
- -
_____
_____
- -
_____

6. Please contact me on the telephone this evening.

_____
- -
_____
_____
- -
_____

Name _____.

Spelling Test

Directions: As your teacher reads your words, write each spelling word on the blanks below.

1) _____

2) _____

3) _____

4) _____

5) _____

6) _____

7) _____

8) _____

9) _____

10) _____

11) _____

12) _____

13) _____

14) _____

15) _____

Name: _____

Fact and Opinion

Directions:
Write your opinion. Then, write four facts to support your opinion. Write your conclusion in the last box.

My Opinion:

FACT #1:

FACT #2:

FACT #3:

FACT #4:

Conclusion:

Name:_____

To the Moon

Directions:
Write your spelling words in the correct category based on the spelling pattern. Underline the spelling pattern in each word.

-oo	-ew	-ue

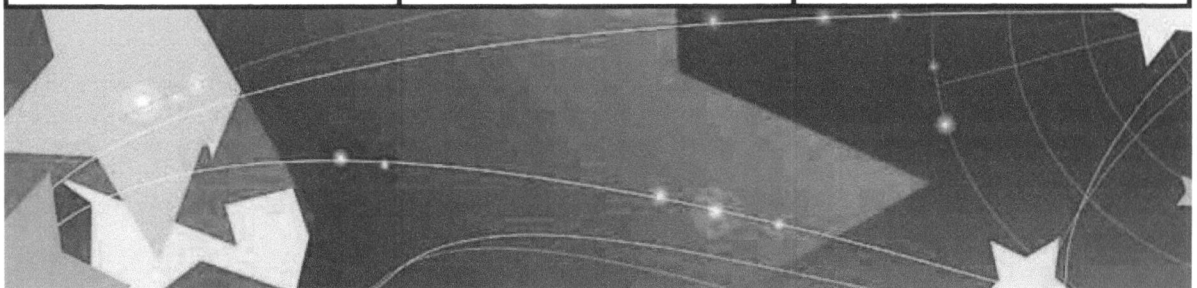

Name _____.

Spelling Test

Directions: As your teacher reads your words, write each spelling word on the blanks below.

1) _____

2) _____

3) _____

4) _____

5) _____

6) _____

7) _____

8) _____

9) _____

10) _____

11) _____

12) _____

13) _____

14) _____

15) _____

Name:_____

The Future
Phonics: Multiple Syllable Words

Directions: Write the syllables of each word.

1. timeline _____ / _____

2. future _____ / _____

3. rapid _____ / _____

4. technology _____/ _____ / _____ / _____

5. sister _____ / _____

6. wonder _____ / _____

7. button _____ / _____

8. second _____ / _____

9. cabin _____ / _____

10. computer _____ / _____ /_____

Name: _____

The Future
Spelling

Directions: Complete the table.

📖 Read the Word	✍️ Write the Word	✏️ Draw a Picture
timeline		
robot		
future		
sister		
button		
cabin		
computer		
dinner		
counter		

Directions: Write a sentence for each word below.

1. development

_____
_____
_____
_____

2. rapid

_____
_____
_____
_____

3. technology

_____
_____
_____
_____

4. wonder

_____
_____
_____
_____

5. second

_____
_____
_____

6. update

_____
_____
_____
_____

Name _____.

Spelling Test

Directions: As your teacher reads your words, write each spelling word on the blanks below.

1) _____ 9) _____

2) _____ 10) _____

3) _____ 11) _____

4) _____ 12) _____

5) _____ 13) _____

6) _____ 14) _____

7) _____ 15) _____

8) _____

The Future
Reading: Poetry

Directions:
Complete each box using the poem from our lesson.

What words rhyme?	What line is repeated?

Why does the poem have rhyming words and repeated lines?

What is the beat? Why is there a beat? **How does the poem make you feel?**

What is the poem about?	Create an illustration for the poem.

Name:_____

Making Plans

Directions: Complete the boxes below based on your topic for the writing assignment.

Setting: Where is the story taking place?   **Characters:** Who or what is in your story?

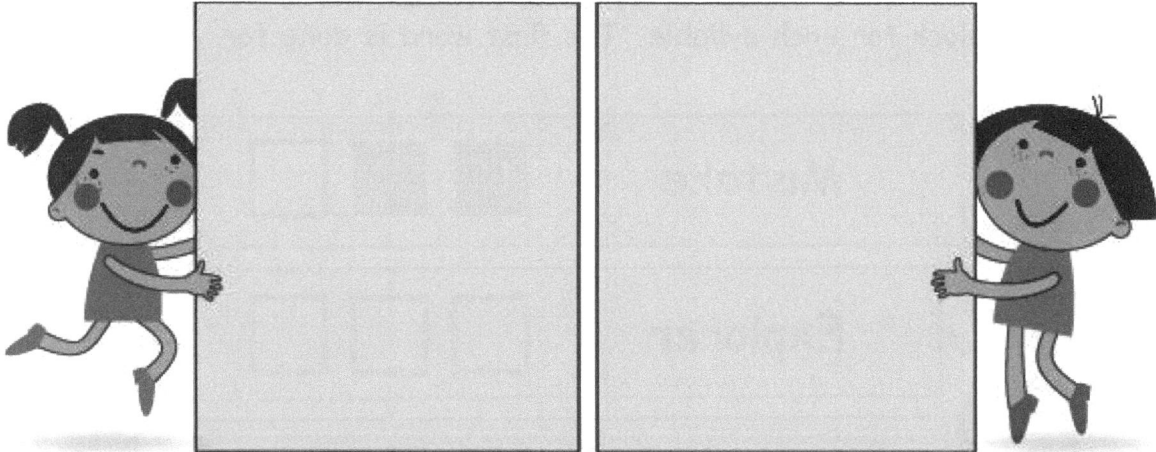

Problem: What is the challenge or obstacle the character faces?

Events: What does the character do to try to solve the problem before arriving at the solution?

Solution: How does the character solve the problem?

Making Plans
Phonics

Directions: Count the number of syllables for each word.
Color in a block for each syllable. The first word is done for you.

Mistake	■ ■ ☐
Explorer	☐ ☐ ☐
Adventure	☐ ☐ ☐
Journey	☐ ☐ ☐
Backpack	☐ ☐ ☐
Grandmother	☐ ☐ ☐
Nobody	☐ ☐ ☐
Hiking	☐ ☐ ☐

Making Plans
Grammar: Prepositions

Directions: Read each sentence. Circle the preposition and underline the noun or pronoun it connects to the sentence. Draw a picture of the sentence in the box.

The rainbow was above the green grass.

Under the table was the box.

The cup of milk is on the counter.

The dog was behind the family.

Making Plans
Phonics: Multiple Syllable

Directions: Write the syllables of each word.

1. spider _____ / _____

2. sadly _____ / _____

3. napkin _____ / _____

4. grandfather _____/ _____ / _____

5. hiking _____ / _____

6. another _____ / _____/ _____

7. alone _____ / _____

8. mistake_____ / _____

9. explorer _____ / _____/ _____

10. nobody_____ / _____ /_____

Name: _____

Spelling - Making Plans

Rainbow Words

Directions:
Please choose three different colored pencils. Write each spelling word three times using each color.

spider   _____   _____   _____

shiver   _____   _____   _____

sadly   _____   _____   _____

napkin   _____   _____   _____

another   _____   _____   _____

nobody   _____   _____   _____

grandmother _____   _____   _____

grandfather _____   _____   _____

hiking   _____   _____   _____

journey   _____   _____   _____

backpack _____   _____   _____

adventure _____   _____   _____

explorer   _____   _____   _____

alone   _____   _____   _____

mistake   _____   _____   _____

Name _____.

Spelling Test

Directions: As your teacher reads your words, write each spelling word on the blanks below.

1) _____

2) _____

3) _____

4) _____

5) _____

6) _____

7) _____

8) _____

9) _____

10) _____

11) _____

12) _____

13) _____

14) _____

15) _____

Making Plans
Reading: Problem/Solution

Directions: Cut out the strips on the second page below. Read the examples of problems and solutions related to our story this week. Then, identify if they are examples of a problem or a solution. Paste them in the appropriate sections.

PROBLEM:

SOLUTION:

Your hiking partner is tired and wants to go more slowly after one mile. You want to run and improve your time.

Talk to your partner and agree ahead of time on how long to walk or run. Make sure you are both at the same level of fitness. If you are already on the hike, talk to each other about a plan that fits both of you for the rest of the hike.

Create a plan of where you want to hike. If you change your mind, talk to each and together pick a new stopping spot.

You plan to hike to the waterfall only, but your partner wants to hike all day by going to the river and back.

After 2 hours of hiking, you realize that you aren't sure how to get to the waterfall.

Read the map ahead of time. If you get lost, have a compass available to help you find your way.

Pack a bottle of suntan lotion in your backpack, along with water and other supplies. If you forget anything, ask your partner.

The sun is hot, and you can see that your skin is beginning to turn red after being outside for a few hours.

Check the weather forecast ahead of time. Just in case, you could include a small rain poncho in your backpack.

You are half way into your hike when it begins to rain. You forgot to bring a rain poncho or umbrella.

Name: _____

Asking Questions
Writing: Rough Draft Cause and Effect

Directions:
Brainstorm cause and effect by completing the boxes below.

Cause: Instead of rain, what do you wish would fall from the clouds?
This could be sprinkles, stuffed animals, or cupcakes.

Draw a picture of what you wish it would "rain."

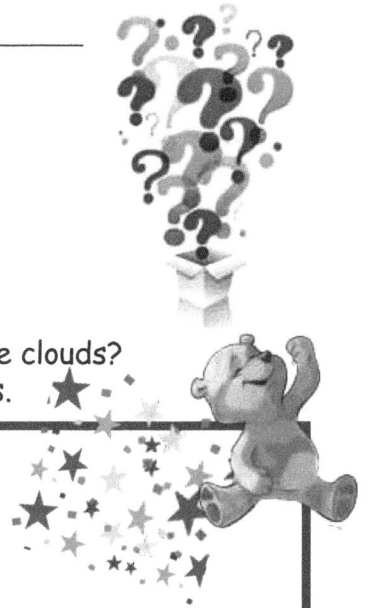

Effect: Draw a picture of what happens as a result of it raining your chosen item.

What does the town look like with your "rain" everywhere?

Characters: Who/What is your story about? Include details.

_____
_____
_____
_____
_____
_____

Setting: Where and when will your story take place?

_____
_____
_____
_____
_____
_____
_____

Problem: Write the problem your character faces. This will most likely have to do with your effect. Is there too much of your "rain?" What will people do with all the "rain?"_____
_____
_____
_____
_____
_____

Solution: How does your character solve the problem?

_____
_____
_____
_____
_____
_____

Name: _____

Asking Questions
Phonics - Silent Letters

Directions: Read each word aloud. Find the silent letter at the beginning of the word. <u>Underline</u> the silent letter.

wrist

wrap

knight

write

wrong

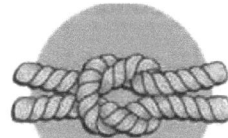

knot

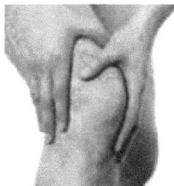

knee

wreath

Name: _____

Asking Questions
Grammar: Complete Sentences

Directions: Read each group of words aloud.
Write if it is a run-on, complete sentence, or fragment.

1) A perfect day _____

2) The girl scored a goal at her hockey game then the team went out for ice cream.

   _____

3) I like to dress up as a chef. _____

4) My baby sister is turning one she is having a birthday party on Saturday.

   _____

5) We will go shopping for a gift. _____

6) Colored the pig pink. _____

7) My parents bought a new car. _____

8) We all went to the beach I brought a shovel and a bucket my favorite thing to do there is to swim in the ocean.

   _____

9) My friend bought stickers for us to share she gave me three and she kept two.

   _____

10) The dog barked loudly at the mailman.

   _____

Spelling Test

Directions: As your teacher reads your words, write each spelling word on the blanks below.

1) _____

2) _____

3) _____

4) _____

5) _____

6) _____

7) _____

8) _____

9) _____

10) _____

11) _____

12) _____

13) _____

14) _____

15) _____

Asking Questions
Reading: Cause and Effect

Directions: Look at the pictures shown. Create the missing cause or effect by drawing a picture in the empty box. Then, write a sentence telling about your picture of the cause or effect.

CAUSE:

They landed on the moon.

EFFECT:

CAUSE:

EFFECT:

It created a lot of traffic.

The cow played the guitar.

Name: _____

Sequential Order

Directions:
Think about a time that you were afraid. Explain the events that led to you being afraid. Why were you afraid? What did you do to solve this problem? Complete the boxes below.

Characters:
Draw a picture of your characters.
(coaches, you, animals, etc.)

Setting:
Where and when does your story take place?
_____
_____
_____
_____
_____
_____
_____
_____
_____
_____
_____

Rising Actions: What events led to you being afraid?

1 ⇒ _____
_____
_____

2 ⇒ _____
_____
_____

3 ⇒ _____
_____
_____

Problem: What were you afraid of?

_____
_____
_____
_____
_____
_____
_____
_____
_____
_____

Solution: What made you not afraid any longer?

_____
_____
_____
_____
_____
_____
_____
_____
_____
_____
_____
_____

Name: _____

Phonics:
-le Letter Combination

Directions: Identify the syllables in the –le words below. Write the syllables of each word ending with –le. Remember, words that end in –le often have a consonant followed by –le as a syllable.

1. apple _____ / _____

2. bubble _____ / _____

3. bottle _____ / _____

4. handle _____ / _____

5. middle _____ / _____

6. puddle _____ / _____

7. jungle _____ / _____

8. people _____ / _____

9. little _____ / _____

10. uncle _____ / _____

Name: _____

Staying Put
Grammar-Adjectives

Directions:
Think of adjectives to describe each picture. Remember, an adjective describes a noun or pronoun. Write down at least two adjectives to describe each picture.

Ice Cream Cone	Pumpkin	Car
1._____	1._____	1._____
2._____	2._____	2._____

Coat	Beach	Snow
1._____	1._____	1._____
2._____	2._____	2._____

Flowers	Tree	Mountain
1._____	1._____	1._____
2._____	2._____	2._____

Name: _____

Spelling - Staying Put

Rainbow Words

Directions:
Please choose three different colored pencils. Write each spelling word three times using each color.

able _____ _____ _____

apple _____ _____ _____

bubble _____ _____ _____

bottle _____ _____ _____

title _____ _____ _____

handle _____ _____ _____

middle _____ _____ _____

pickle _____ _____ _____

puddle _____ _____ _____

uncle _____ _____ _____

little _____ _____ _____

jungle _____ _____ _____

table _____ _____ _____

nibble _____ _____ _____

people _____ _____ _____

Staying Put
Reading: Rising Actions

Directions:
Read the examples of characters, setting, rising actions, and problem in "Goldilocks and the Three Bears." Then, cut out each example of a story element and glue it onto the worksheet in the correct box.

Characters:	Setting:

Rising Action 1:

Rising Action 2:

Rising Action 3:

Conclusion:

Directions:
Cut these story elements out and glue them in the correct box on the previous

Bears' house

Goldilocks, Mama Bear, Papa Bear, Baby Bear

She sits in their chairs.

Goldilocks goes into the Bears' house and eats their porridge.

Goldilocks lies in the beds.

The Bears come home.

Name _____.

Spelling Test

Directions: As your teacher reads your words, write each spelling word on the blanks below.

1) _____

2) _____

3) _____

4) _____

5) _____

6) _____

7) _____

8) _____

9) _____

10) _____

11) _____

12) _____

13) _____

14) _____

15) _____

Name: _____

Writing: Brainstorm

Directions: Think about a weekend from your past. Complete the questions below based on that weekend. Add as much detail as possible.

When was this weekend? What season was it?

_____

_____

Where did the weekend take place? Were you at home? On vacation?

_____

_____

_____

Who did you spend the weekend with?

_____

_____

What were the events that happened during your weekend? List at least 3.

1. _____

_____

_____

2. _____

_____

_____

3. _____

_____

What did you taste or feel during the weekend?

_____
_____
_____
_____
_____

What did you hear or smell during the weekend?

_____
_____
_____
_____
_____

What did you see during the weekend?

_____
_____
_____
_____
_____

How did your weekend end?

_____
_____
_____
_____
_____

Spelling - Moving On

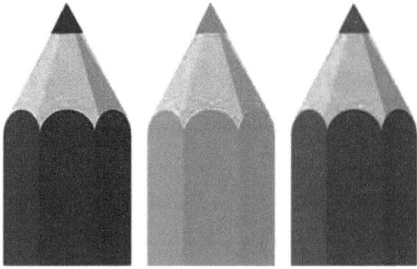

Rainbow Words

Directions:
Please choose three different colored pencils. Write each spelling word three times using each color.

sold _____ _____ _____

fold _____ _____ _____

gold _____ _____ _____

mold _____ _____ _____

poster _____ _____ _____

host _____ _____ _____

ghost _____ _____ _____

cost _____ _____ _____

lost _____ _____ _____

almost _____ _____ _____

frost _____ _____ _____

bold _____ _____ _____

qualify _____ _____ _____

meant _____ _____ _____

excel _____ _____ _____

Moving On
Grammar: Parts of Speech

Directions:
Read each sentence. Identify the part of speech of each **bold** word. Use the word bank to help identify each part of speech. Write the part of speech on the line.

Noun	Pronoun	Adjective
Verb	Adverb	Preposition
	Conjunction	

1. The lady smiled **at** the customer. _____

2. **He** left the game early. _____

3. Cody ate lunch **slowly**. _____

4. My little **sister** will be here shortly. _____

5. I hate riding in a car, **yet** I like flying in a plane. _____

6. I am going to **California** next week. _____

7. The dog **barked** at the stranger. _____

Name _____.

Spelling Test

Directions: As your teacher reads your words, write each spelling word on the blanks below.

1) _____

2) _____

3) _____

4) _____

5) _____

6) _____

7) _____

8) _____

9) _____

10) _____

11) _____

12) _____

13) _____

14) _____

15) _____

Moving On
Reading: Falling Actions and Resolution

Directions: Using our story, "Maria's Goodbye," complete the boxes below. Read each box and decide how it should be labeled. Use the word bank to write the label of each box. One has been done for you as an example.

Word Bank:
Characters   Falling Actions   Setting
Resolution   Rising Actions

....	....
Maria, Principal Mills, Maria's teacher and classmates	classroom and school auditorium

....	Climax
Maria stood on stage to receive an award. Her mom took a picture of the milestone.	Principal Mills told everyone Maria wasn't returning next year.

....	....
A tear ran down Maria's cheek. Students presented her with cards.	The students put special messages in the cards to help Maria transition to a new school. This would help her when she felt sad or lonely.

Visit us on the Web at: www.accelerate.education
ISBN: 978-1-63916-017-4